Puberty

Leon Gray

WAYLAND

First published in 2009 by Wayland
Copyright © Wayland 2009

Wayland, 338 Euston Road, London NW1 3BH
Wayland Australia, Level 17/207 Kent Street, Sydney, NSW 2000

Produced for Wayland by Calcium
Design: Nick Leggett and Paul Myerscough
Editor: Sarah Eason
Editor for Wayland: Jennifer Sanderson
Picture research: Maria Joannou
Consultant: Sue Beck, BSc, Msc

Acknowledgements
The publisher would like to thank the following for permission to reproduce photographs:
Alamy Images: Karel Lorier 8, Photofusion Picture Library/Brian Mitchell 17; Corbis: LWA-Dann Tardif
4; Dreamstime: Marzanna Syncerz 22; Getty Images/Stone: Louis Fox 27; Istockphoto: Chris
Schmidt 28t, Aldo Murillo 28b, Catherine Yeulet 5, 31; Shutterstock: Yuri Arcurs 19, Galina
Barskaya 16, 20, 24, 25, Simone van den Berg 1, 15, Diego Cervo 13, Stephen Coburn 11, Carlo
Dapino 10, Gelpi 6l, iofoto 7b, Glen Jones 23, Emin Kuliyev 26, Patricia Marks 21, Shawn Pecor 14,
Glenda M. Powers 18, Ilya Rabkin 12, Konstantin Sutyagin 7t, Makarova Tatiana 9, Robin Vinson 6r.
Cover image: Shutterstock/Makarova Tatiana

British Library Cataloguing in Publication Data
Gray, Leon, 1974-
Puberty. - (Being healthy, feeling great)
1. Puberty - Juvenile literature
I. Title
612.6'61

ISBN 978-0-7502-5896-8

Printed in China

Wayland is a division of Hachette Children's Books,
an Hachette UK company.
www.hachette.co.uk

Contents

What is puberty?

Puberty is the time when your body changes, as you go from being a child to an adult who can have children of their own. Everyone goes through puberty. It is a completely natural and healthy part of growing up.

Usually, puberty starts between the ages of eight and 13 for girls, and ten and 15 for boys. But it does not really matter how early or late you start to go through puberty. Your body will start to change exactly when it is ready!

Healthy hints

Puberty does not happen overnight. It is a gradual process. Some people go through puberty faster than others. It is not important how quickly or slowly you go through it – everyone catches up with each other in the end.

Roller-coaster ride

Puberty brings about lots of changes. Your body will grow and change shape, and you will also start to have different thoughts and emotions. Your mood can change from one extreme to the other. It can be a bit of a roller-coaster ride!

If you are worried about growing up, try talking to a parent or adult about it.

Nothing to worry about

Some people worry about all the changes that happen during puberty. They may worry that they look different from other people who are the same age as them. They may feel confused about the strong feelings they have.

If you are worried about anything, it really helps talk to someone you can trust, such as a parent or teacher. They will be able to help you work through your concerns.

Finding out about puberty before it starts will help you to understand what is about to happen, and make you realise that puberty is normal.

Puberty is an exciting time – you and your friends are growing into young adults.

Healthy hormones

Your body is full of natural, healthy chemicals, called hormones. From when you are born to when you are old, hormones help your body to work as it should. Growth hormones tell your body to get bigger. Sleep hormones tell you when you are ready to go to bed. Hormones play such a big part in your body that you could not live without them.

Puberty hormones

Hormones are responsible for helping you through the process of puberty. Special puberty hormones tell the different parts of your body to grow and change shape. They cause lots of other physical changes, too. Without puberty hormones, you would be just like Peter Pan – you would never grow up!

Compare a photograph of yourself now with one taken when you were younger. How have you changed?

Puberty hormones not only change your body, they also change the way you think and the way you feel about yourself and other people. Sometimes, during puberty, hormones may cause mood swings, which might make you feel happy one minute and upset the next. Do not worry – these emotional changes will settle down over time.

Hormones cause the differences we see between men and women.

Boys and girls

Different hormones work on different parts of the body during puberty. The main puberty hormones are oestrogen, progesterone and testosterone. Boys and girls have all of these hormones in their bodies – but in different amounts. Girls have more oestrogen and progesterone and boys have more testosterone. This is what makes girls and boys look and act differently when they go through puberty.

Amazing fact

The brain is the body's control centre. It tells parts of your body, called glands, to make different hormones. The glands then release the hormones into your blood. The hormones can then act on different parts of your body.

The growth spurt

One of the things people might say to you during puberty is how tall you are getting. Hormones cause a growth spurt during puberty and people grow at a much quicker rate than normal. Some young people can gain more than 10 centimetres in height in one year! By the end of puberty, most people are close to the height they will be as adults.

Growing pains

Because they are growing so quickly, some children have growing pains as they go through puberty.

Growing pains give you a sore and uncomfortable feeling – mainly in the legs. Although they can be annoying, growing pains are not serious. There is nothing to worry about, and they will pass in time.

If you have growing pains, you can help to relieve the pain by stretching and rubbing the sore area. It is also a good idea to use a heat pad. If the pain is very uncomfortable, ask an adult if you can take a painkiller, such as ibuprofen.

Resting can help you to feel better if you have growing pains.

Changing shape

Hormones not only make people get taller during puberty, they also cause their bodies to change shape. Both boys and girls gain weight. Boys' muscles get bigger, and their shoulders become broader. Girls become curvy, as their hips become wider and they start to grow breasts.

Changes in your shape, size and weight during puberty are perfectly normal and healthy. They are taking you on your way to becoming an adult. Do not feel tempted to cut down on food or to do too much exercise to stop growing bigger. This can be very bad for you.

Feel proud of all the changes you are going through during puberty!

Not to worry

Healthy Hints

During puberty, many young people feel self-conscious at times. If people make comments about changes to your body do not worry – they are not laughing at you or thinking that you look odd!

Body hair

The hormones that make people's bodies grow and change shape during puberty also cause changes in the amount and thickness of their hair. During puberty, hair starts to grow on parts of your body where there was no hair before.

Hair everywhere

You have had hair on your head since being a baby, but during puberty you grow hair elsewhere, too. You soon get used to this new hair.

Nearly everyone has hair on their arms and legs. When you are a child, this hair is often so fine that you can hardly see it. When you go through puberty, it gets thicker and darker. New hair grows under your arms, too. At first, this is thin and light, but it gets thicker as you get older.

During puberty, new, thicker hair also grows around the genitals. This is called pubic hair. When it first grows, it is thin and light. Later, it gets thicker, darker and curlier.

Many girls choose to shave the hair on their legs and under their arms.

Facial hair

You may have noticed that men have hair in places that women do not! During puberty, boys grow hair on their face, chest and back. This is because boys have more testosterone than girls.

Facial hair often starts with a soft, thin moustache on the upper lip. Later, this hair gets thicker, and hair also starts to grow on the cheeks, chin and neck. Towards the end of puberty, boys often need to shave their facial hair, unless they want to grow a beard.

Everyone is different

Body hair is nothing to be embarrassed about. Everyone has it and some people have more than others. Just how much hair you have often depends on how much hair your parents have.

Amazing fact

An average hair grows about 1.5 cm every month.

Some boys start to shave their faces during puberty.

KK376907

Spots and acne

During puberty, different hormones cause the skin to produce an oily substance called sebum. If the skin produces too much sebum, it can make people's hair greasy. Washing your hair more often washes the greasiness away. Too much sebum can also lead to spots, which can last throughout your teenage years.

Spotty skin

Most people get some spots, especially in the early years of puberty. They often appear on the face, the top of the chest and the top of the back. This is perfectly normal and nothing to worry about. If you look around you, you will see that many of the people about your age have spots, too.

A bigger problem

Spots usually come and go during puberty but, sometimes, they develop into acne. Acne occurs when the skin's pores are blocked with oil and dirt. This makes the pores become swollen. Acne can make the skin feel very sore and uncomfortable. Fortunately, there is a lot you can do to treat the condition.

Acne can be treated. If you are worried about spots, talk to your doctor.

Amazing fact

The body needs sebum to keep the skin soft. Sebum also makes body hair waterproof.

What to do

The best way to deal with spots and acne is to drink lots of water and eat healthy food. Wash your face twice a day using just a mild soap and warm water. Do try not to squeeze spots, especially if they are red and sore. This will make them much worse, and could lead to an infection.

If spots become too much of a problem, it is possible to buy special products from the pharmacy to treat them. You can buy special soaps and creams, for example. The pharmacist will be able to advise you on the best product for you. A doctor will give you medication for acne. Ask for help, there is no need to suffer in silence.

Regular washing helps to keep extra sebum at bay.

Breasts and bras

One of the more obvious changes for girls during puberty is that their breasts develop. This can be an exciting time, and many girls look forward to wearing their first bra.

Starting to grow

When the breasts start to grow, the nipples may get darker and stick out more. A small swelling will start to grow under them. This might feel a little bit tender at first, but it will soon settle down.

Sometimes, the swelling may appear under only one nipple at first. Do not worry – you will find that the other one will catch up quickly!

As the breasts develop, the whole area around the nipple gets bigger and rounder. Sometimes, one breast may grow a little faster than the other. This is perfectly normal, and the breasts will eventually even out.

No one person is exactly the same size and shape as another. It is normal to be different.

Fast or slow

Some girls' breasts start to grow before their friends' breasts. This can make them feel self-conscious and embarrassed. They may think that everyone is looking at them. They may be teased if they are the first girl at school to wear a bra.

Everyone changes at different rates during puberty. All girls will develop breasts, because this is a natural part of growing into a woman. But this will happen only when a girl's body is ready – and not before. Teasing is often a sign that people are jealous that other girls are wearing a bra before them. But they should not be concerned, because it will not be long before they are wearing a bra, too.

Ask to be measured by a shop assistant before you start shopping. Bras should be the right size and fit comfortably.

Shapes and sizes

Breasts come in lots of shapes and sizes. Breast size often runs in the family and it is not important. Whether you have large or small breasts, when you are an adult, you will still be able to feed your baby breast milk, if you want to.

A good fit

Healthy Hints

Always make sure that you wear a bra that fits you properly. Many bra shops will measure you and help you buy the right bra.

Having periods

During puberty, our bodies grow and develop in many ways. The process takes us from being a child to becoming an adult who can have children of our own.

An important part of puberty for girls is having periods. Some girls start their periods when they are nine; others may not start until they are 17. Remember, your periods will start when your body is ready.

Why do women have periods?

Women's bodies all have eggs, which can develop into babies when they are fertilised by sperm from men's bodies. Eggs are stored in a woman's ovaries. Once a month, an ovary releases an egg. If the egg is fertilised, it travels to the woman's uterus, where it can develop into a baby. The uterus fills with blood to nourish the growing egg. If the egg is not fertilised, the woman has a period. During the woman's period, the blood from the uterus flows out of her body.

Having periods does not stop girls from doing everyday things.

Sanitary towels and tampons

A period usually lasts between three and seven days. During this time, women use sanitary towels or tampons to absorb the blood from the uterus. Whether you use towels or tampons, it is very important to change them every two to four hours. That way, you will always feel clean and fresh.

You can choose from lots of kinds of sanitary towels and tampons.

Period pains

Sometimes, periods may feel a little uncomfortable. You may have a backache or a stomach ache. You may feel more tired than usual, or a bit moody. These feelings do not last for long and they will soon pass.

You can make yourself feel more comfortable by putting a heat pad on your back or stomach. If you feel upset, talk to your mum or to another trusted adult. They will help you to feel better.

Boy things

Puberty is an amazing time, with lots of changes that prepare our bodies and minds to become an adult. As with girls, some changes for boys prepare them to be able to have children of their own one day.

Size doesn't matter!

During puberty, hormones make a boy's penis and testicles grow. The penis gets longer, and the testicles get bigger and start to produce sperm. Sperm can fertilise an egg from a woman's ovaries to make a baby.

Sometimes, boys get embarrassed about their penis size. They may think it is too small or too big. Remember, penis size is nothing to worry about. Whether a penis is big or small, it will still allow a man to have children when he is ready.

Many changes during puberty prepare a boy to become a father.

Wet dreams

Sometimes, during puberty, boys get an erection when they do not want to. This can be annoying, but it will soon pass. Sometimes during the night, sperm can leak out of the penis when you are asleep, too. This is called a 'wet dream'. Erections and wet dreams are perfectly natural parts of growing up. Never feel worried or embarrassed. These things are simply part of the process of becoming a man.

Deep talker

Another change that takes place in boys during puberty is that their voice gets deeper. This happens because hormones help to make the voice box get bigger. As it grows, you can see it start to stick out at the front of your throat. People often call this the Adam's apple. A girl's voice box is much smaller, and it does not stick out in the same way.

As a boy's voice box grows, his Adam's apple starts to show.

Up and down

Healthy Hints

During puberty, a boy's voice can sometimes sound a bit squeaky. Do not worry, your voice will soon settle, as your voice box adjusts to its new size.

Confusing times

Puberty is a time of great change for boys and girls. Different hormones not only change the way you look, but they also change they way you think and feel.

Puberty hormones can create some strong emotions in girls and boys. One minute, you might feel happy. The next minute, you might feel sad or angry. Many young people find it difficult to understand and cope with these emotional changes.

Puberty has its ups and downs, but it is an exciting time, too.

If you are finding puberty a difficult time, do not worry – you are not alone. Most of the people about your age will feel the same way at some stage. When things seem hard, try to remember – these feelings will not last for ever.

The way you are

Some of the physical changes that happen during puberty may make you feel embarrassed or self-conscious. These feelings can be worse if you think that you are different from others.

Try not to spend too much time comparing yourself to other people. Everyone goes through puberty at different times and different rates. In the end, everyone ends up as an adult. Just make the best of the amazing journey into adulthood.

Making friends

Girls and boys often make new friends as they go through puberty and grow older. Sometimes, a girl and boy like each other so much that they become boyfriend and girlfriend. This is a new kind of relationship. Being a boyfriend or a girlfriend also prepares young people for the loving relationships they will have as adults.

Trusting others

Healthy Hints

If you ever feel really worried or unhappy, talk to your parents or another trusted adult.

It might seem strange if your best friend suddenly starts spending lots of time with someone else. You might feel hurt and left out. Try to see it from both sides, if you can. Your friend is just enjoying the exciting experience of growing up. And, one day, you will also have a girlfriend or a boyfriend of your own.

Having good friendships makes growing up a lot easier.

21

Family matters

Being independent is a natural part of growing up. It is how people prepare to look after themselves as adults. During puberty, as you grow up, you may feel a strong desire to become more independent. Sometimes, this can lead to arguments with family members.

Family is an important part of everyone's life. Our families are often a great source of love, support and fun. Young children like to follow the instructions from their parents or other caregivers. This is how they learn.

As you grow older, you develop your own thoughts and opinions. During puberty, hormones make these feelings much stronger. You may want more freedom and personal space. This is normal. Just make sure you work things out with the people who love and care for you.

Good to talk

Healthy Hints

Remember that your parents or caregivers want only the best for you. It can be hard sometimes, for them to accept that you are growing up. But you can work things out if you keep talking!

Your parents went through puberty, too! It might help to talk to them about how you are feeling.

A brother or sister can be one of the best people to support you through puberty.

Feeling trapped

During puberty, there are times when you feel quite grown-up, but also times when you still feel like a child. One minute, you might want to be left alone but, the next minute, you want some company. This can feel very confusing. It can be confusing for other family members, too!

Communication

Communication is the key to happy relationships, not just in the family but with your friends, too. This means listening as well as talking. It involves respecting other people's views, as well as your own. Always talk to your family and friends about how you feel. They all have different experiences of life. They can help you to make the right choices about your own life.

Healthy eating

During puberty, your body goes through many different changes on the outside and on the inside. Eating healthy food is important during this time of change.

The best for your body

Your body needs to eat food regularly. Breakfast is the most important meal of the day. It will give you the energy you need to kick-start your day. Eat healthy meals and snacks regularly during the day. Eat when you are hungry, but do not keep eating when you already feel full.

Try to always eat a variety of healthy foods. Your growing body needs plenty of carbohydrates, such as cereal, bread and pasta, for energy. Fruit and vegetables give you lots of vitamins. Meat or vegetarian alternatives to protein, such as beans, are great for your muscles. Dairy products, such as cheese, milk and yoghurt help to keep your bones strong and healthy.

If you feel very tired and low, improving your diet may help.

Avoid having too many fatty or sugary foods and drinks. These are high in calories, which can make you put on too much weight. And they do not contain many nutrients. They are best saved for occasional treats, rather than eaten every day.

Feeling fat

Everyone gains some weight during puberty. Your body needs to grow bigger, and change its shape and size, as you grow up to become a healthy, happy adult. Some people feel fat during puberty. Do not worry about this. You will become slimmer again as you grow taller.

Eating problems

Some people think they are fat when, really, they are thin. This can lead to serious eating problems, such as anorexia and bulimia. These conditions can be dangerous. Eating problems can affect both boys and girls.

Healthy Hints

Just talk

If you are worried about your weight, talk to someone you can trust, such as your parents.

Eating healthily will help you to cope with the changes of puberty.

Keep on moving

Taking exercise is very important during puberty. It helps you to be fit and healthy. Exercise also builds strong muscles and bones. It can even prevent conditions such as heart disease and depression.

Keeping in shape

Puberty is the perfect time to keep your body in good shape. Your muscles get stronger during puberty, so you may find that you can do more sport and are better at it.

Happy times

Experts have found that the brain releases special chemicals, called endorphins, when you are active. Endorphins make you feel happy. When you exercise, it helps you to relax. You forget about anything that might be worrying you, including any concerns you may have about puberty. These good feelings carry on even after you have finished doing your exercise.

Swimming is a great exercise – it keeps you fit and is relaxing, too.

What to choose

The best kind of exercise gives you stamina and strength, and helps to keep your body flexible. There are lots of different types of exercise to choose from. Everyone can find an activity they enjoy!

Team sports, such as football and hockey, are great ways to make friends. If you prefer to exercise alone, you could try swimming or cycling. You are more likely to stick at a sport if it is something you find fun to do.

Playing a team sport is sociable. It is also very satisfying when you win!

Healthy Hints

One hour a day

Everyone should try to do one hour of exercise each day to stay fit and healthy.

Time to sleep

During puberty, your body works extra hard. Try to get at least ten or 11 hours' sleep a night. This will give your body time to rest and recover.

Puberty diary

Why not keep a puberty diary to record some of the major changes taking place during this exciting period in your life?

Keep a record

Use a notebook to record measurements such as your height, weight, chest size, hip size, waist size and skin condition. Set up the pages in rows and columns to record the data. You will need one page for each month. You could even paste in passport photos every month or two to show how you are changing.

How are you feeling?

Your emotions are an important part of the puberty process, too. Write down how you feel at the bottom of each page.

Date		
Height		
Weight		
Chest size		
Hip size		
Waist size		
Skin condition		
Emotions		

Quiz

Take the puberty challenge!

1 **Every time your aunt sees you, she tells you are getting tall. Do you:**

a) Ignore her; you hate people commenting on the way you look?
b) Be patient; she only says it because she cares about you?
c) Tell her to leave you alone; it's none of her business?

2 **You have started your period and you do not want to do P.E. at school. Do you:**

a) Tell your mum you feel too ill to go to school, and stay at home?
b) Do P.E. anyway; you may not feel like it, but it will make you feel better?
c) Go to school, but 'forget' to take your kit in, so you do not have to take part?

3 **You are a boy, and your friend has started to grow a light moustache. Do you:**

a) Feel jealous, because you have not got any facial hair yet?
b) Don't say anything; it's a normal part of puberty – and you'll catch up, in time?
c) Laugh at him and tell him he looks silly?

4 **You have a few spots on your face. Do you:**

a) Feel self-conscious and embarrassed; you think you look stupid?
b) Wash your face regularly, and ask your parents to buy some special cream, if they get worse?
c) Squeeze them to try to get rid of them?

5 **You want to go to the park on your own, but your parents or caregivers say that you are not allowed. Do you:**

a) Pretend you are doing some homework with a friend, and sneak out to the park without telling them?
b) Tell them that, now you are getting older, you want to be more independent – but listen to them, and work something out that everyone is happy with?
c) Run up to your room, shouting at them that you hate them?

Answers

Mostly **bs**: Well done! You have learned a lot about puberty. You know ways to look after yourself, and to respect and get on with others during what can be a roller-coaster time. You can find out even more by reading different books and websites, if you want to!

Mostly **as** or **cs**: You have some way to go before you pass the puberty challenge. Remember, there is a lot going on during puberty. It will help you to find out as much as you can, so you know how to handle it. Keep reading this book; it will give you lots of information and ideas! And talk to your parents or caregivers – they will be able to give you helpful advice and support, too.

Glossary

acne A skin problem that results in blocked pores and painful spots.

anorexia An eating disorder that occurs when people restrict what they eat to prevent weight gain.

bulimia An eating disorder that occurs when people eat a lot of food, then make themselves sick.

carbohydrate Food such as rice and pasta that gives the body energy.

calories Units that measure the amount of energy in food.

depression A condition some people have that makes them feel unhappy for a period of time.

eggs Cells in a woman's body, from which babies may develop if they join with a sperm cell from a man.

endorphins Chemicals in the brain, which can make people feel happy.

erection When a penis becomes erect.

fertilised When the man's sperm cell joins with a woman's egg cell.

flexible When parts of your body can bend easily without breaking.

genitals The private parts of the body between the legs.

glands Parts of the body that produce different chemicals.

hormones Chemicals that tell the body to do certain things.

muscles Tissues in the body that can tighten and relax so you can move.

nutrients Substances found in food, which are good for your health.

oestrogen A type of hormone, found mainly in women.

ovary The female reproductive gland. The ovaries release eggs.

penis The male reproductive organ. The penis delivers sperm into a woman's body.

periods Monthly cycle in women when blood flows out of the uterus.

pores Very small holes in the skin.

progesterone A type of hormone, found mainly in women.

sanitary towel Soft, absorbent material worn by women between their legs during their period.

sebum An oily substance that keeps the skin and hair waterproof and stretchy.

sperm A cell in a man's body. If a sperm joins with a woman's egg a baby may be created.

tampons Small cylinders that fit inside a woman's body during her period.

testicles The two round parts of the body below a man's penis. The testicles produce sperm.

testosterone A type of hormone, found mainly in men.

uterus Part of a woman's body where a baby develops before birth.

vitamins Substances found in food, which are good for your health.

Find out more

Books

Healthy Body: Puberty and Your Body
Alison Cooper
(Wayland, 2007)

Health Issues: Puberty
Susan Elliot-Wright
(Wayland, 2007)

Problem Page: Me and My Body
Judith Anderson
(Franklin Watts, 2005)

Problem Page: Me and My Feelings
Jillian Powell
(Franklin Watts, 2008)

Hair, There and Everywhere
Jacqui Bailey
 (Franklin Watts, 2008)

Sex, Puberty and All That Stuff
Jacqui Bailey
 (Franklin Watts, 2005)

Websites

This website has lots of information about puberty, including interactive images that show how boys' and girls' bodies change during puberty.
www.bbc.co.uk/science/humanbody/ body/index.shtml?lifecycle

This website is packed with excellent articles that explain what happens to your body as you grow up. It includes lots of fun games and experiments, and you can watch movies, too.
http://kidshealth.org/kid/grow/ body_stuff/puberty.html

This is a fun, interactive website that tells you all about the changes that occur during puberty.
www.thehormonefactory.com

Index